This

TIME&
ETERNITY

is presented to

_____

by _____

message _____

_____

_____

date _____

JOSHUA MILLS

TIME&ETERNITY

Taking Authority
Over Your Day!

Time & Eternity: Taking Authority Over Your Day!

ISBN: 978-0-9830789-3-7

Item # BK-16

Copyright © 2012 by Joshua Mills

Published by NEW WINE INTERNATIONAL, INC.

In USA: PO Box 4037, Palm Springs, CA 92263

In Canada: 47-20821 Fraser Hwy, Suite #450,

Langley BC V3A 0B6

Toll-free 1-866-60-NEW-WINE

Online 24/7 www.NewWineInternational.org

Cover design by Carl Butel at www.deepimage.net.au

Internal design by David Sluka at www.hitthemarkpublishing.com

Printed in the United States of America

Endorsements

JOSHUA MILLS IS AN AUTHENTIC MAN OF GOD who walks in impeccable purity and integrity in both doctrine and practice. I was deeply blessed when I read *Time & Eternity* and you will be too. Joshua takes a deep revelation of a powerful kingdom mystery and presents it in such a clear, practical, and digestible way. Believe me when I say, "you will never be the same after you read this wonderful book."

PATRICIA KING
Founder XP Ministries
Maricopa, Arizona
XPministries.org

JOSHUA MILLS' NEW BOOK WILL EQUIP YOU in a practical way to live beyond the constraints of time. How will that benefit you? You will live longer and enjoy greater peace, health and prosperity. More importantly, you will accomplish your full destiny!

SID ROTH
Host, *"It's Supernatural!"*
www.sidroth.org

THE LIFE AND POWER OF GOD FLOWS from His throne eternally. We live in temporal, discrete moments of time. How can we cross over to the realm of God's glory? In

Time and Eternity, Joshua Mills reveals many gold nuggets of insight into God's ways with simple steps you can practice to merge your time with God's eternal life. If you live by these principles you will have a greater understanding of God's ways, experience God's glory, fulfill many divine purposes for your life and maximize the value of your time. This is a book to definitely to take TIME to read.

JOAN HUNTER
Author of *Power To Heal* and *Healing The Whole Man*
Joan Hunter Ministries, Pinehurst, Texas
www.joanhunter.org

I WANT TO RECOMMEND JOSHUA'S BOOK *Time & Eternity* to you. Your spiritual life will be greatly enriched and your soul will be stirred and encouraged. These are days when we must know how to function as the Body of Christ with true divine authority. This book will give you insights for understanding how to take your place in advancing the kingdom of God.

BOBBY CONNER
Eagles View Ministries
Bullard, Texas
www.bobbyconner.org

THERE HAS NEVER BEEN SUCH A TIME AS THIS in the history of mankind wherein the Lord is revealing His mysteries and secrets as we enter the end of the age. In *Time*

& Eternity Joshua Mills has captured the essence and nature of revelation the Lord desires to release at this exact point in time, which will bring greater insight into the lives of every reader who hungers and thirst's for the greater glory of the Lord. Its' contents will be empowering to you!

PASTOR PETER NASH
Senior Pastor, Frontline Worship Centre
Red Deer, Alberta
www.frontlineministries-int.com

MANY CHRISTIANS, LIKE ME, are constantly saying, "I never have enough time." Joshua Mills has written this powerful and pioneering book to challenge believers to learn, by faith, to pull from the realm of eternity, enabling us to fully live each day in God's very highest purpose. His teaching stretches us to go beyond the norm, both practically and spiritually, and fulfill our destinies by redeeming the time that is so precious in these last days. This radical book takes the current signs and wonders understanding to a whole new perspective. Read it and let the Holy Spirit empower you to live life in a whole new dimension.

PASTOR PHIL WHITEHEAD
Senior Pastor, Chiswick Christian Centre
London, UK
www.chiswick.cc

IN A DAY WHEN MORE AND MORE CHRISTIANS are struggling with anxiety, depression, and fear, and are under pressure because of all the demands on their time, Joshua Mills has come with a fresh word from God that teaches us how to walk in authority and live in blessing and peace. This book will change your life!

BILL PRANKARD
Evangelist, Bill Prankard Evangelistic Association
Ottawa, Ontario, Canada
www.bpea.com

Other Books by Joshua Mills

31 Days To A Breakthrough Prayer Life

31 Days To A Miracle Mindset

31 Days Of Health, Wealth & Happiness

Advanced School Of Miracles

Atmosphere

Co- Powerful Partnerships In Marriage

Heaven Invading Hollywood

Into His Presence – Praise & Worship Manual

Living Grace

Ministry Resources 101

Personal Ministry Prayer Manual

Positioned For Prosperity

Powerful Encounters In The God Realm

School Of Miracles, Volume I

School Of Miracles, Volume 2

School Of Signs & Wonders, Course I

School Of Signs & Wonders, Course II

Simple Supernatural

Simple Supernatural Study Guide

Third Day Prayers

Available online 24/7 at:
www.NewWineInternational.org

Table of Contents

From His eternal posture the Lord created time as one of His great mysteries to serve His purposes. However, God is not bound by our human limitations and perceptions.

Foreword
by Paul Keith Davis

For many years I have observed with interest and appreciation the ministry of Joshua Mills. He has introduced the supernatural dimension of God's nature through various revelatory insights and profound signs and wonders with humility and integrity. Recently while in a conference together I heard Joshua share phenomenal Kingdom mysteries concerning "time and eternity." What he shared struck deep within me with a heavenly witness. I knew these were key biblical principles essential for our day.

Someone once said that God dwells in eternity; perhaps it would be more appropriately stated that eternity dwells in Him. From His eternal posture the Lord created time as one of His great mysteries to serve His purposes. However, God is not bound by our human limitations and perceptions.

Instead, we are expanded through His eternal attributes accessed through His promises and nature.

Albert Einstein is considered one of the greatest scientific minds in modern history. He is quoted as saying, "the only reason for time is so that everything doesn't happen at once." Elsewhere, time is defined as the continuum of existence created by God by which our future becomes our present and moves into our past.

Regardless of the definition we choose to embrace, the reality is that God has created time for His purposes in order to reveal Himself to mankind and unveil His eternal attributes. Like all of His creation, the Lord has established laws that govern time and existence. Even so, those laws are also subject to His dominion, rule and pleasure.

As promised, the Lord is raising up ministries in this hour to apprehend hidden mysteries that have been set apart for the "End of Time" generation. A pure revelatory anointing is being delegated to present day prophetic voices, like Joshua Mills, which will launch the Bride of Christ into the "greater works" and access to the unseen realm that supersedes the time and space continuum.

This truth was typified and foreshadowed when Israel departed Egyptian bondage under God's covenant blessings. It was as though the natural effects of time were suspended while they lived under the cloud of His glory and the fire of His presence. The Bible tells us there was not one feeble person among them. Not only that, neither their clothing, nor sandals deteriorated; and it was said of Moses that his eyes did not grow dim nor was his strength abated at the age of 120. The natural effects of time were suspended by God's glory.

I once had a revelatory encounter in which I saw the Lord Jesus standing at a distance holding a ruler or measuring staff. He was gazing intently at it when I asked, "Lord, what is that?" Without diverting His focus from the ruler, He answered, "Time, for time is measured."

At that moment I intuitively knew that He, from His eternal posture, viewed all of time simultaneously. I also recognized that time is a tool in His hand used to unfold His plans, purposes and pursuits. Furthermore, I also came to understand that we were strategically placed at precisely the right moment in time for a specific function and destiny. The apostle Paul emphasized this in Acts 17:26 saying, *"and He made from one man every nation of mankind to live on all the face of the earth, having determined their appointed times and the boundaries of their habitation."*

The Lord has emphatically spoken to me on a number of occasions about His quickening power and the wonderful promises reserved for the time of the Latter Rain. These promises will be apprehended and demonstrated by champions in the Last Day Army. That is why I was particularly interested in the revelations I heard Joshua sharing concerning "Time & Eternity" and God's willingness to redeem and restore time in our generation. I recognize in him and the message he carries, the stewardship of key mysteries that will launch this generation into its high calling and ultimate destiny.

Some years ago I was in Dallas, Texas, preaching in a large church on the ministry and anointing of El Shaddai. I shared that God first appeared to Abraham by this name in Genesis 17:1. In my message I quoted the definition of this divine name as the "All Sufficient-One; the many-breasted One," as I had read in dictionaries. There happened to be a professor of Hebrew in the meeting. He approached me after the meeting and asked, "Can I help you a little with your understanding of El Shaddai?"

He said, "What you shared about El Shaddai is not inaccurate, it's just incomplete." He continued, "The truest definition of El Shaddai is, 'I am the God of utter ruin and devastation and I am here to do for you what you cannot do for yourself.'"

Although I appreciate the understanding given by many authors concerning the definition of El Shaddai as "the all sufficient One" or the "many breasted One," we must also consider what many Jewish writers have suggested concerning this divine attribute as much more far-reaching than our present understanding discloses. As one Jewish scholar put it, "It [the name El Shaddai] belonged to the sphere of salvation, forming one element in the manifestation of Jehovah, and describing Jehovah, the covenant God, as possessing the power to realize His promises, even when the order of nature presented no prospect of their fulfillment, and the powers of nature were insufficient to secure it. The name which Jehovah thus gave to Himself was to be a divine pledge."[1]

How perfect and applicable that definition is for the circumstances in Abraham's life at the time of this visitation. The patriarch had been given the promise of a son through Sarah; however, Abraham was one hundred years old when the Lord appeared to him as El Shaddai. As Paul tells us in Romans 4, his body was as good as dead and Sarah's womb was no longer fruitful.

Abraham was not able to fulfill the promise now in His own strength. God did for him what he could not do for himself. He quickened Abram and Sarai's mortal bodies and restored their youth through His covenant blessing, and their names were changed accordingly. El Shaddai reversed the effects of time on their natural bodies to allow His promises to be fulfilled. Genesis 18:11-14 tells us:

> *Now Abraham and Sarah were old, advanced in age; Sarah was past childbearing. Sarah laughed to herself, saying, "After I have become old, shall I have pleasure, my lord being old also?" And the LORD said to Abraham, "Why did Sarah laugh, saying, 'Shall I indeed bear a child, when I am so*

old?' Is anything too difficult for the LORD? At the appointed time I will return to you, at this time next year, and Sarah will have a son.

Shortly after this blessing, Abraham traveled to a southern country ruled by a king by the name of Abimelech. This king exercised his royal right of bringing beautiful women into his harem to make them his concubines. Now Abraham is once again faced with the same dilemma he encountered in Genesis 12 some twenty-five years before. Sarah's great beauty became a threat to his safety, so he lied, claiming that she was his sister. God's jealousy for His promise prohibited the king from cohabiting with Sarah.

How was it that Sarah was now so beautiful after it was stated previously that she was advanced in age and now ninety? God's quickening power restored her beauty and superseded the natural effects of time. He restored her youth!

Furthermore, we also discover in the latter years of Abraham's life following the death of Sarah, his marriage to Keturah. He was now approximately 140 years of age and fathered six sons through her. Clearly, the blessing of El Shaddai quickened Abraham and Sarah into a youthful state that allowed these tremendous blessings even though their natural age would have otherwise been prohibitive.

If such wonderful things could transpire in an inferior covenant sealed with the blood of bulls and goats, how much greater the covenant blessings sealed with the blood of Jesus

Christ. That is precisely what Joshua Mills reveals to us in his book, *Time & Eternity*.

I pray that as you read this book your heart will be provoked and your eyes illumined to the reality of the eternal realm and the Lord's willingness to redeem, restore and supernaturally utilize time for His purposes.

Paul Keith Davis
WhiteDove Ministries
Foley, Alabama

*As you seek Him, you will find Him, and
when you find Him, the benefits of the
Glory will begin to manifest in your life.*

Introduction

Spiritually speaking, we move at the speed of light. Your *acceleration* is always determined by your *illumination*. Always. And revelation is always available.

The Bible says that Jesus Christ is the light of the world (John 8:12). Heaven doesn't need the light of the sun or the moon because heaven has the light of Jesus Christ. It is illuminated by the brilliance of His glory (Revelation 21:23-24). Because Jesus is constantly shining, revelation is always present. There is a constant illumination in the realm of heaven that causes revelation to constantly pulse forth, but you must be willing to receive it. Revelation can only be obtained by passionate pursuit.

When you receive revelation, it demands activation in order to cooperate with that illumination to produce a manifestation in your life. Are you ready to manifest something new? Draw on the realms of heaven for the revelation that is about to come forth, because as you receive it, it will produce a blessing in your life. I'm telling you, beyond a shadow of a doubt, it's going to produce a blessing. I have already experienced it working in my life. I have already seen it beginning to function—opening up doors I never dreamed possible.

I believe the Holy Spirit will move on you even as you read the revelation on these pages. You are going to feel it in your spirit. You may read something that you've never been able to verbalize, or you haven't had a scriptural proof for, but you've known it in your spirit. It was on the inside; you knew it, but you never knew how to explain it or how to identify with it. This word will make your heart leap, and you will feel a witness to it in your spirit. The Bible says, *"Every matter must be established by the testimony of two or three witnesses"* (Deuteronomy 19:15; 2 Corinthians 13:1), so I believe God is going to confirm what I share in you.

John 16:13 says,

> *"But when he, the Spirit of truth, comes, he will guide you into all truth."*

Let Him do this for you. Ask the Holy Spirit for discernment and revelation concerning what He is saying. I tell you this: when the revelation of God comes forth, that revelation is intended to take you to a new elevation in God. Every single revelation in God is intended to lift you higher than before.

22

You Travel at the Speed of Light

Did you know that you travel at the speed of light? Get this in your spirit: you travel at the speed of light. So in essence, you travel at the speed of revelation.

―――――――

You travel at the speed of light.
So in essence, you travel at the
speed of revelation.

―――――――

The Bible says this: we go from one degree of Glory to the next degree of Glory. God does not want to take you down. God wants to lift you up. If a supposed revelation comes, and you find yourself falling back in the Lord, then that is not a right revelation. That is not a revelation from God. But when you receive a revelation from God you receive a true, genuine revelation from the Holy Spirit that should propel you beyond your years of natural ability or understanding. It should cause a hunger inside of you for the Word of God. You will feel a desire to pursue God's presence, spend more time with Him, and seek His face. As you seek Him, you will find Him, and when you find Him, the benefits of the Glory will begin to manifest in your life.

I want to take you somewhere in these pages. I want to take you into the realm of the Spirit. Every time the Glory of God shows up, it shows up to take us places. The Glory of God never comes so that we will remain in the place we have always been; instead it comes to advance us to the next level.

The Glory of God always comes into our presence to shift the atmosphere around us and to change our perceptions. The Glory of God always comes to move us. When the cloud of Glory came to the people of Israel, it moved ahead of them so that the people would move with the cloud. The Bible says the Israelites would follow the cloud, and that the cloud would lead them. The Glory was always moving. And sometimes, it would settle over a place where there was a specific purpose for them. And as the cloud hovered, then the Israelites received from the cloud in that location.

But when the Glory comes, it never leaves you in a place of lack. It never leaves you in a place of sorrow. It never leaves you in a place of grief or unfruitfulness. When the cloud of Glory comes it always comes to move you into a place of producing more fruitfulness than you have ever produced before. We are moving into the realm of eternity where time will no longer hold you down.

Expect radical transformation as you read this book. New realms of the Glory will open to you within these pages as eternal truths of Scripture come alive in a new way. Get ready, because God is about to do something marvelous in you, for you, and through you!

Chapter 1

Making the Very Most of Your Time

Teach us to number our days aright, that we
may gain a heart of wisdom. – Psalm 90:12

There is a connection between making the most of your time and growing in your revelation of heaven. Does that alarm you? Perhaps you have always wrestled with time. You may already feel defeated, so the thought that your revelation of heaven is somehow connected to your time management skills scares you.

Someone once said, "Our days are identical suitcases. All are the same size, but some people can pack more into them than others." Have you ever felt that way? Have you ever looked at others' lives and wondered how they accomplish so much, while try as you might, you accomplish so little in comparison? If this describes you, then I have good news for you.

You do not have to live with the way your suitcase has always been packed. There is a way to make it fit many more blessings! Yes, you read that right. You no longer need to live with the limited resources you have known all your life. What is the key to packing more into your suitcase? Eternity. Eternity is the key to expanding your days, increasing your productivity, experiencing profound joy, and being able to enjoy life the way God intended.

We see throughout the Scriptures that some of the ancients learned how to push the boundaries of time. Do you want to learn how to remove obstacles of limitation that have been hindering you for years and begin living with more time on your hands?

If your answer is yes, then I am going to show you how. There is revelation that can be found within the pages of God's Word that will accelerate your productivity, increase your fruitfulness, expand your outreach, and bless you beyond measure!

Time is a Tool

We need to understand that God created time as a tool for us. Time is not supposed to work against us or hinder us in any way because God created time to work for us. Proverbs 11:9 (KJV) says,

Through knowledge shall the just be delivered.

So let us get God's revelation on this very important tool that He created.

Time is not supposed to work against us or hinder us in any way because God created time to work for us.

Have you ever said:

"I don't have enough time."

"I need more time."

"Time is running out."

"I wish I had another day to work on this."

"If only time would stand still."

"Time seems to be flying away."

After I found myself saying these things, the Lord began to speak to me about time. The demands on our ministry are many. I consistently travel all over the world with a busy itinerant speaking schedule. Last year alone we hosted nine different ministry schools in various places around the globe. I traveled all over, from Vancouver to Hawaii to Bangkok and Colombo. This past year I went to more than fifteen nations. One of those nations was Australia, where I spent almost an entire month ministering. When we go to the nations, we don't just go for a few days; we go for an entire week or longer.

Yet in spite of all this, I have been able to write seventeen books and manuals over the past two years, as well as many ministry cards and teaching resources. I've also been able to as well as spend time in the studio recording a new worship CDs. After so much was accomplished this past year, I looked back and said, "God, how was I able to do that except for the revelation you gave to me about time?"

God Created Time for Our Good

Genesis 1:14-18 says:

> *And God said, "Let there be lights in the expanse of the sky to separate the day from the night, and let them serve as signs to mark seasons and days and years, and let them be lights in the expanse of the sky to give light on the earth." And it was so. God made two great lights – the greater light to govern the day and the lesser light to govern the night. He also made the stars. God set them in the expanse of the sky to give light on the earth, to govern the day and the night, and to separate light from darkness. And God saw that it was good.*

The Lord put lights in the sky – the sun, moon, and stars. Why? To separate the day from the night. God created day and night. These lights were also to *"serve as signs to mark seasons and days and years."* So here we can see that these lights were not only a clock for day and night, but also the calendar as well. God put the entire calendar in place on the fourth day of creation.

Verse 18 gives us the understanding of why the lights are in the sky: to govern the day and the night, to separate light from darkness. And God saw that this was good.

David spoke about creation in Psalm 8:3-4:

> *When I consider your heavens, the works of your fingers, the moon and the stars, which you have set in place, what is man that you are mindful of him, the son of man that you care for him?*

David is saying, "Compared to the great lights that govern time, who am I that you would think of me?" But he doesn't stop there. Verses 5-8 continue:

> *You made him a little lower than the heavenly beings and crowned him with glory and honor. You made him ruler over the works of your hands; you put everything under his feet: all flocks and herds, and the beasts of the field, the birds of the air, and the fish of the sea, all that swim the paths of the seas.*

Look at that again: *"You made him ruler over the works of your hands."* In other words, "You have given man dominion over the works of Your hands." David made it very clear that God gave man dominion and authority over all creation. From the beginning of the Scriptures we can see that time is something that God created on the fourth day. It's important to understand that time has a beginning and it has an end (see Matthew 24:35; Mark 13:31; Luke 21:33). The bible even speaks about the end of the "time line" within the book of Revelations (See Revelation 21:4). Time is a created substance and through Jesus Christ, God has given us dominion over it.

Jesus Restored Lost Dominion Over Time

When God said, "It was good," He was speaking of His creation, and everything was paradise. Man and woman ruled with dominion over all that God had created. But Adam and Eve's sin separated them from God and the dominion authority God had entrusted to them.

Jesus Christ came as the second Adam (See 1 Corinthians 15:47). Why? To restore to us what was rightfully ours in the beginning—right relationship with God, others, and the earth He created. After conquering sin and death, Jesus said,

> *"All authority in heaven and on earth has been given to me." – Matthew 28:18*

Authority over what? Over all creation, which includes time.

God created physical things—sun, moon, stars—in order to create time. God created time in the beginning. God created time as a tool for us to use, not as a weapon to be used against us. Yet many of us have felt as though time is working against us. The clock is ticking against us. We are always battling with time. But the Bible says that God has given you dominion over His creation, over every created thing. Everything is under your feet (Ephesians 2:6; 1:22), and that includes the realm of time.

God has given you dominion over His creation, over every created thing. Everything is under your feet, and that includes the realm of time.

There are No Seasons in Eternity

God resides in the realm of eternity and is not bound by time. He exists within your past, present and future all at the same moment. According to Revelation 22:13, He is Alpha and Omega—the Beginning and the End. He has always existed from eternity to eternity. In the realm of heaven, there is no day and no night, but only eternity. And eternity is the realm of continuous illumination and life.

Eternity has always been, and it will always continue to be. God brings the eternal past and the eternal future into the present now. This realm of eternity is constant. There are no ups and downs. There are no good times and bad times because there is no time. It is a constant realm of goodness, blessing, provision, and holiness. It is a constant realm of miracles, wholeness, prosperity, and the Glory of God. The realm of eternity is constant!

During a time of prayer, the Lord recently said to me, "Joshua, I am inviting you out of your season into a new dimension." He didn't say, "I am inviting you into another season." He said, "I am inviting you out of your season into a new dimension." You see, many of us go through seasons. We have good seasons and bad seasons, watered seasons and dried seasons. We have seasons of prosperity and seasons of poverty. We have seasons of health and seasons of sickness. We have seasons when we feel like we are on the top of the mountain, and then we have other seasons when we feel like we are at the bottom of the valley. We have seasons where we have lots of friends, and we have seasons when we cannot find anyone. Some seasons we feel very loved and other seasons are times of tremendous loneliness, and depression tries to take control.

But in the realm of Glory, there is no season. The realm of Glory is a constant realm of goodness. Some might point out that the Bible says to know the times and the seasons; 1 Chronicles 12:32 says that the sons of Issachar understood the times and the seasons. Do you realize that is Old Testament? They didn't have Holy Spirit living on the inside.

But we do—the very essence of His constant presence, Jesus Christ, the hope of Glory, the hope of eternity.

We must be careful not to open the door to the enemy's attack simply because we see that attack as only another "season of life." What did Jesus pray?

"Your kingdom come, your will be done on earth as it is in heaven." – Matthew 6:10

Is the earth going to experience seasons? Absolutely. Do you have to be a part of the season? Absolutely not.

Is the earth going to experience seasons? Absolutely. Do you have to be a part of the season? Absolutely not.

Enter the Eternal Realm of God's Goodness and Glory

This is an amazing revelation. The Bible says that you are in the world, but you don't have to be a part of its ways. This means that you do not have to be subject to the instability, the inconsistency, the ups and the downs, and the roller coaster rides—feeling great one day and the next day feeling like you want to die. You can be in the world, but you don't have to be a part of its ways.

Everybody else is screaming, *"Economic despair, economic recession. I feel like I'm going into a depression."* Not me. Philippians 4:19 says, *"My God shall supply...."* It doesn't matter whether I'm having a good day or a bad day, whether you've been nice to me or not. I am going to be supplied for; I am going to be provided for. In God I experience a constant flow of blessing.

There is a constant realm of goodness in the realm of Glory. That is the realm that I *receive,* because it is the realm I *perceive.* Whatever you perceive, you'll receive. If you see goodness, you will receive it. If all you see is poverty, you will receive it. This is why the Bible says to be careful, little eyes, what you see. If your eyes are filled with light, your whole body will be consumed with light. If your eyes are dim, and filled with darkness, then the darkness will start to creep into your life (Matthew 6:22-23).

But I tell you this: God doesn't want you to walk in seasons of despair, seasons of wilderness, seasons of loneliness, seasons of fear, or seasons of depression. There is a better way for you. God is inviting you out of your season into a new dimension. That dimension is the eternal Glory of God—the eternal realm of God's goodness.

Some may say, "Well, we don't have enough time for that to happen." You're right, you don't. There will never be enough time for you to do what you are called to do. But God is not asking you to live from the realm of time. He wants you to rise up into a new dimension and begin to live as an ambassador of heaven. The Bible says that you are a citizen of another realm (Philippians 3:20), of a place that is not ruled by time. Everything you need is available in that realm, and you can be in this realm, releasing another realm. You can walk in time but be a part of eternity. In the realm of eternity, things can happen that could never happen in the natural. This is why Matthew 19:26 says, *"With God, all things are possible."*

God is not asking you to live from the realm of time. He wants you to rise up into a new dimension and begin to live as an ambassador of heaven.

If time was water in a glass, it's like the glass has been tipped over. Time is running out. We are coming to the end of time. Time is running out, but eternity is running in. There is a collision of two realms right now—the realm of eternity and the realm of time. This is why, as we gather in His name, and in the presence of the Holy Spirit, God begins doing things that could never happen in time. Suddenly God begins to work miracles that time has declared impossible. Stop looking to time to give you something that only God can provide.

No matter if you have one day to live, or one hundred years, stop worrying about time and begin to rise up into the realm of eternity. Time is a tool that God has given to you to help you manifest the realities that come from the realm of eternity. In the Glory you will succeed. It does not matter what you need. God has supplied for all of your needs (Philippians 4:19). Every need is already provided for in the realm of eternity—now it's a matter of bringing it into time.

Supernatural Time Management

Ephesians 5:15-16 says:

> *Be very careful, then, how you live—not as unwise but as wise, making the most of every opportunity, because the days are evil.*

Supernatural time management begins with natural responsibility. Many people waste time simply because they are ignorant of the simple tools that would make them more efficient in completing their tasks. I want to give you some practical time management keys that have helped me to be responsible with my time. These are some useful tips that I have learned over the years:

• **Analyze Your Time**: What's Working, What's Not Working, What's Most Important?

It is necessary to discover how you work best with the gift of time that you've been given. Do you find that you will achieve more if you give yourself a daily list? Or are you able to accomplish more through spontaneous activity? The constant, little tasks that clutter our days can be the biggest killer of time. Purge your schedule of unnecessary activity. Recognizing what is most important will enable you to stay focused on the task at hand. When you recognize what matters most, it will save you from smaller distractions that come and go.

- **Catch the Vision**

Give yourself clear goals and priorities—write them down and make them clear for yourself and others to understand. The Bible tells us to write down the vision so that we might be able to accomplish it successfully (Habakkuk 2:2).

- **Make a Daily List**

Nothing wastes time like the tyranny of the urgent. When we let our days assign our tasks for us, we fall back into reaction mode, fighting whatever fires spring up and making little to no progress toward what really matters. Write down your necessary tasks at the beginning of each day and prioritize them according to urgency and the time it will take to complete them. Then pray over your list, as I will teach you throughout the rest of this book.

- **Practice Time Mapping**

I began using this principle several years ago when I noticed that several of our ministry workers were unable to successfully accomplish their tasks on time. Time mapping has proved to be a successful way to track where your time is being spent—as well as recognizing ways that your time could be used more appropriately. You can practice this by allotting specific spaces in your daily schedule for the core activities of your life or work duties. Assign time slots of fifteen, thirty or sixty minute "zones" to things such as personal time, family life, spiritual disciplines, work, relationships, finances, education, etc. Larger zones can then be broken down into smaller chunks. For example, a sixty-minute "work" zone can be subdivided into fifteen-minute slots for things like returning calls, answering e-mails, and scheduling appointments. If you color code your system you will find you are able to visually balance the things that are most important to you.

- **Assign Any Task That Somebody Else Can Do!**

Do not waste time doing something that someone else could do for you. You've heard the phrase, "Divide and conquer." I prefer the phrase, "*Unite* and conquer." If you are in a position to delegate at work, training and empowering others to do the work will multiply your time and efforts. If you have children, they can contribute by helping with the laundry, dishes, and cleaning. Look around, see who's on your team, and help them unite with you get the job done.

- **Understand Your Energy Cycles**

  Begin to work with time—not against it. When you begin to put these various suggestions into practice, keep in mind that this is not a race against the clock! Time is your servant—it was created by God to work for you. It will be important for you to recognize your energy cycles in order for your time-mapping and other practical tips to work at their fullest potential. If you recognize that you are most tired after a long day of work, it would be a good idea for you to place your high-energy activities (i.e. exercise) at the beginning of your day as opposed to late in the evening. Through the years I have discovered that I am at my creative peak during the late hours of the night. So, I have often worked to schedule my writing time during those hours when I know that I will work my best. This enables me to be more productive, instead of sitting at my computer with writer's block.

- **E-mail**: Use the Rescue RAFT Method (Reply To It, Assign It, File It, Trash It)

  E-mail can be a black hole for wasted time if we do not watch ourselves carefully. Without discipline, we will waste valuable time by reading through the same e-mails multiple times trying to find the information we need. Cluttered in-boxes eat precious time as we look for that one e-mail we need among the hundreds we have neglected to file or delete. Cut this waste from your life. Determine to read an e-mail just once and then take the appropriate action on it: Reply to it, Assign it, File it, or Trash it.

If you are not already practicing these things in your life, I encourage you to get started today! But even beyond these natural ideas, remember to cover your days in prayer. When you first wake up and before you go to sleep, thank the Lord for giving you wisdom that will allow you to make the most of your time.

Pray With Me

Father, in the name of Jesus, I thank You for creating time to bless me and not to curse me! I choose to take up dominion over time, as You have given it to me. Holy Spirit, please increase this revelation in me so that I may accomplish all that You have created me to do and become all that You have created me to be! Lord, I thank you for your divine wisdom that opens up supernatural "time-slots" in my day and creates useful portals of opportunity. Amen.

Chapter 2

Supernatural Time Reversal

Different people have their own ideas of what a time machine might look like. As a child of the eighties, it looked like a souped-up, stainless steel DeLorean, or a fancy, glass box that would fill the room with billows of smoke and flashing lights. But now, twenty-some years later, I have discovered in God's Word the amazing truth about supernatural time reversal. It is not just some idea of vain imagination—time reversal is a reality that is available for all Christian believers.

I want to share a testimony with you about the way I discovered God's supernatural time machine! At the young age of sixteen, I had an encounter with the Holy Spirit, and my whole life was instantly focused on God. I didn't want to be out of His will for a second. I didn't want to be one step ahead of Him or one step behind. I just wanted to do whatever God wanted.

I left home at the age of seventeen; the day that I wrote my final high school exam. The Lord gave me clear direction on where I was supposed to go, and the next Sunday a pastor asked me to minister and lead worship at his church. I began to minister in music, and at the age of nineteen I moved from Canada to Spring Hill, Florida and became a worship minister at Emmanuel Christian Center.

During this same time, I began traveling to San Diego, California, where there was an extended revival going on with thousands of people being dramatically impacted by the move of the Spirit. I began leading praise and worship at the revival, and the Lord opened up supernatural doors for me to travel to different places around the United States.

I got married at the age of twenty, and at twenty-one I returned to Florida. Six months later I was back in Canada where I had started. Back in Canada together, Janet Angela and I asked God, "Why do we feel like we are in the very same place that we started? We've done all this stuff for years. We've spent all this time and effort, and it feels like we've gone around in a circle, and now we are back at the beginning."

You can probably relate to this feeling. It feels like you're simply going around and around. What is going on? The Lord spoke to me during this time and said, "Sometimes you have to go back to go forward." I didn't understand at first, because the Bible says to keep your eyes focused on the prize that's set before you (Philippians 3:12-14). Just keep on going forward.

⟫-◦-⟪

Sometimes you have to
go back to go forward.

⟫-◦-⟪

Go Back to Go Forward

You see, it's not about going backward. It's about moving forward. In moving forward, we go back to go forward. How does that make any sense? Let me explain by looking at David's encounter with Goliath. David was so absolutely unqualified and ill equipped to overcome the giant Goliath that everybody else was afraid. They were shaking in their boots—they were terrified. But God had His man, and he was only a young man.

The Bible says that David had a sling in his hands. He had a few stones too. We think about David's sling like it was one of those Tom Sawyer slingshots where you pull the elastic band back really far, and when you let go, the rock shoots forward at somebody. But that's not the slingshot David had.

During a trip to Israel a few years ago I saw a slingshot souvenir similar to what David would have used. This slingshot did not have an elastic band to pull back. Instead, it had a small place to hold a rock so that you could spin it around and around and around over your head like a lasso. The Lord showed me that sometimes when we feel like we've been going in circles, it's as if we are in that sling going around and around. We are always moving forward, even though sometimes we end up back at the same place where we started. But with every single cycle, every turn, we are gaining in momentum. There's speed and acceleration, and there's something that is happening in the realm of the Spirit as you go around, around, around.

Sometimes you have to go back to go forward. What's happening is that God is moving you. He is providing momentum and acceleration while you are learning and receiving revelation—revelation that you will need for the days ahead. When the momentum and acceleration get to just the right place, suddenly you are released from that cycle and you are propelled forward. And as the stone went forward, it went directly into the giant's head, and Goliath fell on his face.

You may feel like you've been going around in circles like I've described. But God is about to propel you into the greatest days that you've ever known. You are about to be released forward to hit the very giant that has tried to stand in your way and defeat you. You are about to hit the giant in the forehead, and that giant is about to come tumbling down. Praise God!

Back to the Future

2 Kings 20:1 says:

In those days, Hezekiah became ill and was at the point of death. And the prophet Isaiah, son of Amos, went in to him and said, "This is what the Lord says, 'Put your house in order because you are going to die. You will not recover.'"

What? The prophet said, "You had better put your house in order because you are about to kick the bucket." What an encouraging prophetic word! Well, Lord, thank You for the prophet. Hallelujah, thank God we are not living in the Old Testament! When God gives you a prophetic word today, it's not a word of despair, but it is an encouraging word, a victorious word. Aren't you glad about that?

The prophet said, "You'd better get things right. You are about to die." But the passage goes on saying, "Hezekiah turned his face to the wall and he prayed to the Lord." His response was prayer. Prayer changes things. When you begin to pray to God, He listens. The Bible says He listens to our prayers. Hezekiah prayed (verse 3):

Remember, oh Lord, how I have walked before you faithfully with wholehearted devotion and have done what is good in your eyes.

Then the Bible says that Hezekiah wept bitterly. Some translations say that his tears were great. Verse 4 says:

Before Isaiah left the middle court, the word came to him, "Go back and tell my people, this is what the Lord, the God of your Father, says, 'I have heard your prayer and I have seen your tears. I will heal you. And on the third day from now you will go up to the temple of the Lord and I will add fifteen years to your life. And I will deliver you in this city from the hand of the King of Assyria.'"

Hezekiah asked Isaiah, "What will be the sign?" Did you know that God likes to release signs? Whenever God speaks there are always signs that follow. The Bible says that signs will confirm the Word of God (Mark 16:17-20; Hebrews 2:3-4). In other words, when the sign begins to come, it's a confirmation of the Word of God that has been spoken. Why? Because God watches over His Word in order to see it manifest (Jeremiah 1:12).

Hezekiah asked,

> *"What will be the sign that the Lord will heal me and that I will go up to the temple of the Lord on the third day from now."*

Isaiah replied,

> *"This is the Lord's sign to you that the Lord will do what he has promised: Shall the shadow go forward ten steps, or shall it go back ten steps?"*

Isaiah was asking by the Spirit of God's instruction, "Should time go forward or should time go backward?" Should time go forward or should time go backward? You're kidding me! The Lord says this is going to be a sign for you. Either time is going to go forward or time is going to go backward.

And this is Hezekiah's response:

It is a simple matter for the shadow to go forward ten steps.

Hezekiah meant that the clock always goes forward. So rather than have it go forward ten steps, Hezekiah said, "I want to see it reverse." So the prophet Isaiah called upon the Lord, and the Bible says that the Lord made the shadow reverse ten steps up the stairway. The Lord took the clock and made it go back!

You may be thinking, "There is no way; this is absolute rubbish. I've never heard this before. There's no way we can go back in time." Sorry, too late. I've got a word from the Lord. If you get it in the Word, you can have it. If the Lord did it for Hezekiah, and he was in the Old Testament, the Bible says that what I can experience today is even greater than that Glory. We can experience a Glory greater than that which Hezekiah, or Moses, or even Adam experienced. You can experience a greater Glory (Haggai 2:9).

Through Jesus Christ, we have received a greater Glory. Time went backwards for Hezekiah. Time can go back for you. Hezekiah received two things. First, he received healing. Second, he received a renewal. The Bible says that God added fifteen years to his life. Now how do you add fifteen years to somebody's life?

When you are adding years to someone's life, you are not making somebody older; you are making somebody more youthful. So when the Lord added fifteen years to Hezekiah life, what He was really doing was reversing the prophetic sign that Isaiah received and taking him back to go forward.

The Glory Time Warp

In the Glory realm you can experience a time warp! The Lord is able to take you back to go forward. In the Glory realm, time can be stopped, accelerated, stretched, reversed, and made to work for you. This is scriptural.

⎯⎯⎯≫〇≪⎯⎯⎯

In the Glory realm you can experience a time warp! The Lord is able to take you back to go forward.

⎯⎯⎯≫〇≪⎯⎯⎯

Let's look at Psalm 103:1-5 where one of the benefits is to restore your youth. Verses 1-2 say:

Praise the Lord, my soul; all my inmost being, praise His holy name. Praise the Lord, my soul, and forget not all His benefits.

This is talking about being a people of praise—a people who will worship the Lord. David says three times to praise. As you have a spirit of praise, your praise changes the atmosphere. Praise changes your perspective. And suddenly instead of seeing the problem, your praise begins to show you the solution. As you praise the Lord, you begin to remember the benefits that God has already provided for you through His Word. What are these benefits?

Four Supernatural Benefits of Praise

- **Benefit One: Salvation**

  Verse three says, *"…who forgives all your sins."* The benefit of salvation is foundational for the Christian experience. Jesus Christ was born to a virgin. This is completely impossible in the natural, but completely possible through God. In the realm of time it does not make sense. It does not matter how long a virgin just sits and waits to get pregnant. In the realm of time, it is never going to happen. But the Bible says that the Holy Spirit overshadowed her. Eternity came on the scene and did something that only eternity could manifest. Jesus Christ lived a perfect life and then was crucified. In the realm of time, dead people do not come back to life. In the realm of time, you can wait and wait and wait, but unless there is a touch of God's Glory—unless there is a touch of eternity—the miracle would never happen. But Jesus Christ rose from the dead and provided the way for our sins to be forgiven so we could be in right standing with God. We should not forget the benefit of salvation.

• **Benefit Two: Healing**

Verse three also says, *"And heals all your diseases."* Healing and wholeness is a benefit of God that can only be received from the Glory realm. Praise changes the atmosphere and you begin to remember your benefits. What's that benefit? It's healing! Some people have forgotten. The Bible says it like this: *"Where there is no vision, the people perish"* (Proverbs 29:18, KJV). If you don't have vision for healing, if you don't have the revelation, you will suffer. Just because you haven't seen it does not mean it doesn't exist. Some say healing is not for today. If you don't believe in healing, then you won't manifest the fruit of healing. Some people say, "Well, I believe that God wants me to be sick. He is teaching me a lesson. He's trying to get me to slow down." If God is teaching you a lesson, then why are you taking your medication in rebellion against God? It's illogical thinking. If God is teaching you a lesson, then why aren't you learning your lesson? God doesn't make people sick. God doesn't teach people a lesson by making them sick. God doesn't try to slow down people. Healing is a benefit we must remember!

- **Benefit Three: Redemption From Destruction**

  Verse four says, *"Who redeems your life from the pit."* God redeems your life from the pit. This is deliverance and supernatural protection. It's another provision in the realm of God's Glory. Not only does He deliver you, He *"crowns you with love and compassion."* What an incredible benefit!

- **Benefit Four: Renewed Youth**

  Verse five says, *"Who satisfied your desires with good things."* God desires to satisfy your desires... with **good** things, not just-so-you-can-get-by things. Why? *"So that your youth is renewed."* What does that say? Does it say that the Lord is trying to teach you a lesson by slowing you down with problems? No! He satisfies your desires with good things, so that your youth is renewed. The Bible says that God desires to turn back the time in your life. God desires to lift you up to a realm of eternity that is an ageless, timeless realm. Even in old age you can function as though you were not old in time. When you live from another dimension, it doesn't matter what this dimension is dictating; you can be in the world but not a part of its ways. I have met some elderly people in the natural who are absolutely filled with youthfulness and zest for life. They are walking in divine health.

A few months ago I was at my grandparents' house in Essex, Canada, and my Grandfather asked me, "Joshua, how many fillings do you have in your mouth?" I said, "Grandpa, I don't know, maybe one or maybe two, not very many. But I have some." He said, "My teeth are completely whole. I have never been to the dentist and I have never had one cavity in my entire life." It doesn't matter what time dictates when you live in the realm of eternity. You can live from a different dimension and manifest it here in this realm. The Bible gives us a promise of youth being renewed. Are you ready to go back to go forward?

Age Reversal and Wrinkle Removal

Several years ago I was in the south of France, and the Lord spoke to me, "I'm removing wrinkles from people." When I spoke the word I said, "The Lord is removing wrinkles from people's faces," adding the emphasis on faces. A woman on the front row called out, "The wrinkles I got aren't on my face."

The Lord corrected me through her, and I apologized and said, "I stand corrected. The Lord is removing wrinkles wherever you've got them. He's removing them." When I released that word, God began removing wrinkles, yes, on people's faces, but also on different parts of their bodies.

The Lord also added through a prophetic word that He was removing age spots from people's bodies. Some of the people were curious and asked where that was in the Bible. Well, the Bible says that Jesus is coming back for a church without spot or wrinkle (Ephesians 5:25-27), so you can take that however you want to take it!

If you want, take this word for yourself. I believe that things will begin to transpire in your body as a prophetic sign of what God is doing on the inside—of the changes that He is making, of the new energy that He is giving, of the supernatural strength, of the restoration of time, of the divine appointments that are being reassigned to your life. Receive all that God has for you!

Thirty Years Before the Accident

In one meeting I had in the Midwest, a woman went back thirty years one night! She had been in a car accident thirty years prior. It had messed up her physical body and caused her a lot of grief. The Lord gave me a word of knowledge that somebody was going back thirty years. I declared it, and the Lord watched over His Word to perform it! God actually took her back thirty years to *before* the car accident ever happened! She received complete restoration in her body. Praise God!

Falling Back Up the Stairs

Last year something unusual happened as I was downstairs working in my tool shed. I had the door open to our staircase because Janet Angela had been going up and down the stairs. Suddenly, I heard Janet Angela screaming. I looked out the door and there she was lying on the floor all hunched up. She had fallen down the stairs and had hurt herself badly. Instantly, a holy unction of the Spirit of God rose up within me, and I declared, "In the name of Jesus, I take you back fifteen minutes."

Do you know what happened? Janet Angela looked at me and said, "What just happened?" I replied, "You just fell down those stairs." She told me that the last thing she remembered was being at the top of the stairs, and the next moment sitting at the bottom of the stairs completely unharmed. She didn't remember falling. Not one thing was wrong with her.

Now if you knew Janet Angela, you would understand that she bruises very easily. After I declared, "I take you back fifteen minutes," there was not one bruise, not one scratch— nothing was wrong. It was an absolute miracle.

Slipping Into a Miracle

One winter we were ministering in Stony Plain, Alberta. While the weather was fairly warm for the season, there was still a lot of ice on the pavement around our hotel. One after- noon, my son Lincoln and I were walking back to the hotel. Suddenly, I heard him start screaming and crying behind me. I quickly turned to look and saw that Lincoln had slipped on the ice and fallen onto the pavement. I ran back to pick him up and discovered that his hands and legs were scraped and bloodied.

Instantly, I felt the Spirit of God come on me with faith and I declared, "In the name of Jesus, I take you back five minutes." After I said this, Lincoln looked at me and replied "Dad, I feel a lot better." We went up to the hotel room, and I told him to run his hands under water. When he removed his hands from the water, all of the scratches were gone, and there were no more signs of the accident anywhere on his body! His knees that had been scratched up were instantly healed! We experienced another miracle of taking authority over time.

Time Miracles Happen for an Inuit Lady

A few months ago I was ministering in Quaqtaq, Nunavik, and one of our ministry partners, Lucy Audla was in those meetings. A few weeks later she sent us an e-mail with an incredible testimony. In her e-mail she said,

> Joshua taught us about taking authority over time. Just two days after returning home, my granddaughter Dezerae was outside playing for forty minutes. She came back inside and she was crying hard because she had slipped on the ice and hurt her wrist—her side and her head really hurt. She told me that she could hardly breathe. Right away I remembered the testimonies that Joshua shared and that I could take back time! I prayed that my granddaughter would be reversed forty minutes in time, and suddenly she was fine! She was smiling and she said that all the pain was completely gone! God bless you for that revelation. I wouldn't have known what to do!

Ten-Year Age Reversal

One lady was in my meetings several years ago and she felt that the Lord told her He had taken her back ten years in time. After the meeting she felt younger, more vibrant, and more alive than ever before! When she went to her scheduled doctor's appointment a few days later, the first thing he said when he saw her was, "What happened to you? You look ten years younger!"

Instant Weight Loss

A few years ago I was ministering in Aurora, Ontario, and in the very last night of meetings there were about twenty people that received supernatural weight loss instantly in the meeting. People went down dress sizes and miraculously lost weight that they had been carrying around in their bodies for years. It was quite remarkable to say the least. You know, sometimes you can be standing in a miracle realm, watching everyone else receiving their miracles, and not even recognize that God has a miracle for you too! The day after that meeting was my wedding anniversary, so I spent the entire day with Janet Angela.

One thing I have learned over the past thirteen years of marriage is that Janet Angela loves to shop! So for our anniversary I took Janet Angela to the shopping mall. I wanted to buy her some new clothes for our upcoming trip to Paris. Do you know what happened? As I was walking around the mall, I had to keep pulling up my jeans, because they kept dragging on the ground! Funny thing was, I had just bought the jeans a few weeks prior while I was ministering in Seattle, and so I knew that they weren't too big. Actually, I had purchased a size too small because they were the last ones left, and they were on sale! So it didn't make any sense that they were now too big! As I was walking around the mall that day, I kept thinking, "What is going on with these jeans?" And then suddenly, it hit me—I had been standing in that same miraculous realm for supernatural weight loss the night before, along with all those twenty people that received a miracle, and God had touched me also even though I didn't perceive it at first! I had miraculously dropped two pant sizes over night! We went home, and Janet Angela took a few pictures of me with my oversized jeans. We spent the rest of the evening laughing and rejoicing in the wonderful miracle that God had done!

In the realm of God's Glory, He is able to take you back in time—erasing memories of the past and removing injuries and scars from accidents and abuse. He is able to rejuvenate your body with divine health, healing, and wholeness. There is nothing too difficult for God. Will you receive this miracle today?

Prayer for You

Father, in the name of Jesus, I bless the person reading this book right now. I thank You for removing wrinkles, and I thank You for removing age spots. Lord, I thank You for removing blemishes, warts, and moles. I command them to go in the name of Jesus. I thank You, Lord, that You make all things new in the realm of Your Glory. I thank You for ALL of Your incredible benefits, and for Your complete renewal. I ask that their youth would be renewed like the eagles'. In Jesus' mighty name, Amen!

Jesus Christ came to give you life, and life more abundantly, not only in the heavenly sphere, but also right here on the earth!

Chapter 3

Favor With Time

Faithfulness and obedience to God's Word opens up a "fountain of youth" in our lives (John 4:14). We can see this throughout the Scriptures:

- Adam lived to be 930 years old. (Genesis 5:5)
- Noah was in his four hundreds when he received the instructions to build the ark and was in his six hundreds when the ark floated on the floodwaters. He lived until he was 950 years old! (Genesis 9:29)
- Methuselah, son of Enoch and granddaddy of Noah, lived to the age of 969. (Genesis 5:27)
- Abraham was 175 years old when he passed away. (Genesis 25:7-8)
- God's servant Moses stayed youthful to the age of 120 while retaining 20/20 vision and strength that never departed! (Deuteronomy 34:7)

- Caleb was just as strong in his eighties as he was at the age of forty—full of vigor, courage and ready for battle! (Joshua 14:10-11)

- Countless other biblical figures lived many years to experience a full and rewarding life. Jared lived 962 years (Genesis 5:20), Mahalaleel lived 895 years (Genesis 5:17), Lamech lived 777 years (Genesis 5:31), Shem lived 600 years (Genesis 11:10-11), Eber lived 464 years (Genesis 11:16-17), Enoch lived 365 years (Genesis 5:23), Peleg lived 239 years (Genesis 11:18-25), Terah lived 205 years (Genesis 11:32) and the list goes on.

Why is it that these people could live so long, and yet we are dying so young? Some may talk about a pre-flood environment or defend Genesis 6:3 that says God shortened our life span to 120 years. Regardless, that's still 120! You can live longer because God has a solution for you.

I am not saying that you will not pass on. The Bible says that each person is appointed to die and then face judgment (Hebrews 9:27). But do you know what happens when you face death? Although your physical body may seem corruptible, you do not die. A believer never dies (1 Corinthians 15:55-57)! You will just go from one dimension of living into another dimension of living more abundantly. You transition from living on this side to living on the other side—simply crossing over! But it's important to know that you can live longer on this side if you apply the principles of the Word of God and the Glory of God in your life. Jesus Christ came to give you life, and life more abundantly, not only in the heavenly sphere but also right here on the earth!

Jesus said,

> *"Indeed, the water I give them will become in them a spring of water welling up to eternal life."*
> *– John 4:14*

The eternal life that Jesus is speaking of is not just for the age to come. It's for the here and now! Gloria Copeland says that, "Life is in Jesus Christ, and Jesus is the Word made flesh."[2] It is still as powerful and indispensable as ever. If you doubt it, read the New Testament book of Hebrews. It says that God's Word not only created the world in eons past but it still holds creation together today. Hebrews 1:3 declares that right now Jesus is *"upholding all things by the word of His power."* He is actually keeping the universe on course with His Word. Don't you think He can keep you going? What is more, Hebrew 4:12 tells us that the Word affects us as born-again believers in a real and dynamic way. It is life to us just as it was to the people in Moses' day, because now, as then:

> *The word of God is alive and active. Sharper than any double-edged sword, it penetrates even*

to dividing soul and spirit, joints and marrow; it judges the thoughts and attitudes of the heart.

Psalm 35:27 says,

God takes delight in the PROSPERITY of his servants.

How much God delights in the prosperity of His sons and His daughters! John also said,

Beloved, I pray that you would be in health and prosper, even as your soul prospers! *– 3 John 2*

Your soul is able to prosper in the Word of God. Your mind, will and emotions can receive the truths and realities of God's Spirit. Through this Scripture, John gives you an understanding that God wants this same prosperity to overflow into your physical health and into your entire well-being.

Prosperity at the Right Time

God wants to prosper you, no matter your age, no matter your natural obstacle. The promises of God are yes and amen (2 Corinthians 1:20). Elizabeth received this promise, and it came forth in her "old age," because the prosperity of God extends from eternity to eternity (Luke 1:26-37)!

God said through Isaiah:

Even to your old age and gray hairs I am he; I am he who will sustain you. I have made you and I

*will carry you; I will sustain you and I will rescue
you. – Isaiah 46:4*

This is a promise that God makes to you; that you will
never lack for anything no matter where you are in life. These
verses are an invitation to break the boundaries of "seasons" in life and jump into the eternal dimension of God's
glorious provision!

Healing evangelist Gordon Lindsay has said, "To have
our youth renewed we must satisfy ourselves with the 'good
things' of God. 'Man shall not live by bread alone, but by
every Word that proceeds from the mouth of God' (Matthew 4:4). Physical bread will fail, but the Word of God is
life indeed. Divine health is for those who feast daily on the
'good things' of God's Word."[3]

God Wants to Lengthen Your Days!

Proverbs 3:1-2 says:

*My son, do not forget my law, but let your heart
keep my commands; for length of days and long life
and peace they will add to you. (NKJV)*

This Scripture speaks about God not only lengthening
your years but also lengthening your days. How is your day
lengthened? When eternity is put in the middle of the day, it
extends your time. You can have a longer and more fulfilling

day than anyone else. When eternity enters into your day, you will be able to do more with less!

You can have a longer and more fulfilling day than anyone else. When eternity enters into your day, you will be able to do more with less!

I was in a situation where I was preaching on a week-long ministry cruise, scheduled to return home on Monday. On Wednesday I was scheduled to be preaching in Phoenix, Arizona. From Phoenix I was flying directly to Australia for a month of ministry there. And from Australia I was traveling to Hawaii, where I was scheduled to teach at the Intensified Glory Institute®. There was only one problem: I had not started writing two full courses that I was supposed to teach at the school!

The student manuals needed to be written, printed, and ready for my arrival in Hawaii. I was beginning to wonder how this would possibly happen! That's when God began unfolding this revelation about time and eternity in a greater way for me. I recognized that God wanted to increase my days. All I needed to do was connect to that reality. Suddenly I found myself declaring over my day:

Time and space, get out of my face,

I was created for mercy and grace.

I won't make room for conflict and stress,

I know that I am continually blessed.

The Glory is here and filling my day,

I know that God will have His way.

You can use this declaration to commit your days unto the Lord. Start by declaring:

- You are going to have favor with time. Time is your servant and it is ready to work for you!

- Your day is going to be supernaturally stretched longer with greater productivity.

- You are going to experience divine connections that will save you from unnecessary labor, stress, and expense.

- You are going to be able to accomplish things today that you didn't accomplish yesterday, because God's revelation is expanding within you.

When I began declaring this over my days, suddenly I discovered that not only was I taking care of household tasks, I was able to oversee administrative ministry tasks. In addition to managing the day-to-day stuff, I was able to write the student manuals for two schools within two days.

I don't know whether you just read what I wrote, but I said I wrote material for two whole schools in just two days! This is typically not a quick or easy process. Praise God! I discovered that God has given us dominion over time! You can discover this too!

God Did It for Joshua!

God wants to lengthen your day. How is it possible for God to lengthen your day? Joshua 10 shows us how. I love this. Joshua 10:12 says:

> *On the day the LORD gave the Amorites over to Israel, Joshua said to the LORD in the presence of Israel: "O sun, stand still over Gibeon, O moon, over the valley of Aijalon."*

What was Joshua doing? He was taking dominion over time—the sun and the moon, the day and the night. He was speaking to time. He said, "Time stand still," and time stood still.

God wants to give you favor with time. Joshua was doing it here. Why? In order to win the battle.

You may feel like you've been battling in your life (health crisis, financial problems, family issues, etc.). You may even feel like it's been a constant battle with time. Look at what Joshua did. He simply spoke to it!

So the sun stood still, and the moon stopped, till the nation avenged itself on its enemies...The sun stopped in the middle of the sky and delayed going down about a full day. – Joshua 10:13

The Lord gave Joshua an extra day. If Joshua could experience this favor with time in the Old Testament, how much more, as New Testament believers, can we access this favor? How much more can we—Bible believing, Spirit-filled Christian people who walk, and live, and breathe the Glory—experience these realms of Glory? Hallelujah!

If you've been facing a dilemma and said, "I have major time management problems," I want to tell you God knows how to manage time perfectly. The Bible says that God is the Teacher, and the Holy Spirit will teach you all things (1 John 2:27). Whatever you need to know, God knows how to do it. Whatever you need to be taught, God knows how to teach you.

If you've been having problems with time management, then I want you to make these declarations on the next few pages. If you have said, "I haven't had enough time. Time has been slipping away. I haven't been able to do what I feel like I'm called to do," then begin to speak to time—command it to serve you properly!

Even if time has never been an issue for you, I want you to begin to speak to it now before it ever becomes an issue. If you have been faithful with your time, then God wants to multiply it that much more! If you can succeed with a natural amount of time, then what will abound in your life when the realms of eternity begin to invade time?

Wherever you are right now, I want you to begin implementing this. From this moment on, speak over your days every morning. Just begin giving your day to God, offering it to Him, and ask eternity to fill your day. Ask eternity to lengthen your day.

It doesn't matter if time is running out, because eternity is running in!

It doesn't matter if time is running out, because eternity is running in!

Commanding Favor with Time

God wants to give you favor with time, so speak this over your time and your year right now:

> Father, in the name of Jesus, right now I thank
> You that You desire to give us favor with time.
> Lord, I thank You that You created time. Time is
> a blessing for mankind. Time is not a curse, but
> it is my servant.

Lord, I thank You that You have given us assignments, visions, dreams, and directives. I thank You that You cause eternity to fill my day. That through You, my day would be expanded, lengthened, and stretched, and that I would overflow with ability to do what You called me to do.

Lord, I thank You that no longer will my family be neglected. No longer will my ministries be neglected. No longer will my talents, giftings, abilities, or anointings be neglected. Lord, I thank You for allowing there to be enough time in every day, as eternity invades, for me to do every single thing that You've called me to do.

Holy Spirit, I invite You to teach me all things so that I may become good at managing my time. Show me where I have been wasting time. Show me, give me understanding, and direct me where time could be better spent. Lord, please begin leading and guiding me.

Lord, right now, I thank You for divine, supernatural prosperity in my days, for prosperous days. Right now I am declaring prosperous days! Prosperous days this year, I am going to have prosperous days. Every day will be a prosperous day. I am going to do more this year than I have ever done before. I am going to accomplish more in the kingdom of God this year than I have ever accomplished before. I am going to spend more time with my family this year, paying attention to my children, and to my spouse. I am going to spend more time devoted to the things of God this year than ever before. My businesses will prosper this year. My job will prosper this year. God, I thank you that I am being advanced to new levels. I will enter a new dimension of Glory this year in Jesus' mighty name.

Lord, I thank You for releasing prosperity angels into my days. Prosperity angels, right now, are being released into the calendar. Prosperity angels are being released right now into the time clock.

Now praise the Lord with me: Hallelujah! Hallelujah!! Hallelujah!!!

Chapter 4

Going Forward in Time

The key to experiencing the Glory is understanding the NOW. It is important that we believe in the NOW. We need to start speaking to the now moment. We need to stop putting all of our hope into the future. Speak into the now, and declare God's Word now! 2 Corinthians 6:2 says,

> *For he says, "In the time of my favor I heard you, and in the day of salvation I helped you." I tell you, now is the time of God's favor, now is the day of salvation.*

There is no moment like now. Every miracle you need and every blessing from heaven is available right now. When Jesus Christ was crucified on the cross of Calvary, He shed His blood and said, "It is finished." Every work of God has been finished for you. Healing is yours. Prosperity is yours. Restoration is yours. But you must declare it into the now.

In Hebrews 11:1, the Bible declares that *"NOW faith is..."* Faith is NOW! Begin to put your faith into the now. Don't wait for your miracle to happen in three days, three weeks, three months, or three years from now. The Bible says you will have whatever you believe for, so be it according to your faith (Matthew 9:29; 21:22; Mark 11:24; John 14:13; 15:7; 15:16; 16:24; 1 John 3:22; 5:15).

As you intercede and pray, begin to speak things into the NOW. Romans 4:17 describes God as *"the God who gives life to the dead and calls into being things that were not."* Prophesy them NOW. Speak and declare what you hear the Lord saying NOW. Faith-filled words will help you to overcome, but fear-filled words will defeat you. Your words are the most powerful thing in the universe.

Your words contain the power to create the world that you will walk into tomorrow. Your future is contained within the words you speak today. Your future is always determined by what you believe for NOW! Grab hold of eternity now!

What Are You Expecting?

John 2:1-3 says:

> *On the third day a wedding took place at Cana in Galilee. Jesus' mother was there, and Jesus and his disciples had also been invited to the wedding.*

When the wine was gone, Jesus' mother said to him, "They have no more wine."

Jesus' response to this question was, "Why do you involve me?" He was saying, "Why are you telling me this? Why are you saying, 'They have no more wine?' What are you expecting?"

Let me ask you the same question. What are you expecting? So many of us have been in time and controlled by time for so long that time controls our minds. We've been so influenced by the ways of this world that we have not been influenced by the realm of Glory. We must become accustomed to the realm of heaven. Allow heaven to change your thinking. Open up and receive a miracle mindset. Allow God to change your thought life. As soon as your revelation changes, the manifestation changes.

Allow heaven to change your thinking.
As soon as your revelation changes,
the manifestation changes.

You can't keep doing the same thing and expect a different result. Religion will never provide the miracles. Only Jesus Christ can release the miracles. This life is about growing in relationship with Christ and allowing Him to direct your thoughts, so that the pattern of heaven becomes your pattern—the way that you walk and function.

Mary understood the difference between time and eternity. She understood that there were limits in time. But in the realm of eternity, anything could happen. Remember that she was the virgin who became pregnant in a way that could never happen in a million years. But eternity came on her, and she gave birth to the Messiah, the Anointed One. She knew He was going to be the Lord of the earth, that He was the Savior of the world.

Until this point in time, Jesus had never performed one miracle. But Mary knew that the realm He carried was a realm that defied time. But this day, the third day of the wedding, Mary decided to be done with time. You've got to become unsatisfied with the status quo in order to move into the greater miracles. As long as you are okay with today, you will never move into tomorrow.

As long as you are okay with today,
you will never move into tomorrow.

When Eternity Comes, Time is Erased

Last year, on my way to England, I ministered in Iceland for one night. During the service I prayed for a woman who was experiencing such problems with her arm that she feared it might have to be amputated. But when I laid my hands on her, she instantly received a complete miracle. The feeling came back. She was able to move everything properly. It was amazing! With tears in her eyes, she testified to everybody that God had done a real miracle!

After seeing and witnessing what had happened, a little girl who had a cast on her arm also asked me to pray for her. Just after I laid my hands on her, she asked someone to help her take the cast off her arm. She believed that she had received what she had asked for. The cast came off, and her arm was completely healed. Her mother was crying. She was crying. The church was in tears because of the goodness of God. Miracles began to happen all over the congregation with ease.

The doctor may have said, "It's going to take two months for your arm to heal." But when the Glory of the Lord comes on the scene—when the realm of eternity comes—time is erased. This is the reason why miracles begin to happen in the Glory realm. Suddenly, it's not about time; it's about eternity.

John the revelator moved "ahead of time" and experienced this revelation for himself, as he was invited "out of time" into the dimension of the eternal through an open heavenly portal.

After this I looked, and there before me was a door standing open in heaven. And the voice I had first heard speaking to me like a trumpet said, "Come up here, and I will show you what must take place after this." – Revelation 4:1

Jesus' mother, Mary, was a woman who was familiar with the realms of eternity. She understood the Glory that Jesus carried on His life and she understood the eternal purpose of His destiny. She was unsatisfied with time, and the circumstances that time had been dictating. She realized that Jesus carried a realm of eternity. She knew that if she put a demand on the eternal, then the eternal would begin to manifest. When you get a revelation from God, it demands activation. That activation will create a manifestation. Mary put a demand on the Glory.

Putting A Demand on Eternity

Don't settle for less. Don't settle for second best. Don't wait for time to pass for your answer. Maybe what you really need could never happen in a lifetime. Your situation may be so difficult that a lifetime could not provide the answers or solutions you need. But in the realm of the eternal, one touch of God's Glory changes everything. Put a demand on the Glory realm in your life.

Mary said, *"Do whatever He tells you"* (John 2:5). It's not about time; it's about eternity. So do whatever eternity tells you to do. Jesus only did what He saw His Father doing (John 5:19; 12:49-50), and what He spoke was just what His Father wanted Him to say. Jesus was talking about looking into the eternal and pulling it down and releasing it on the earth. Do whatever the Glory tells you to do. Say whatever the Glory tells you to say. Manifest whatever the Glory causes to manifest. Do not be ashamed or afraid of the Glory of God.

I decided a long time ago that I would not be ashamed or embarrassed about the Glory. It doesn't matter what anyone thinks. Some people think I am crazy. They say I am demonically possessed. They say I'm a freak, I'm a fraud, or I'm performing magic. They say I'm a satan worshipper. But I don't care. I know who I am and, better yet, I know who He is! So do whatever He tells you to do.

What happened when they did what Jesus told them to do? The water turned to wine. The Bible says this event was the beginning of Jesus' miracle ministry. Why? Because it wasn't about time, it was about eternity. Jesus said, *"My time has not yet come"* (John 2:4). It doesn't matter. It's not about time. When you recognize the realm of eternity is present, press into eternity and suddenly you will unlock the door into the flow of God's blessings. Hallelujah!

This is what happened in my own life. When I received a touch from God, it escalated me into my destiny! It positioned me into my future. I no longer waited for something to happen. When I received a touch from eternity, it happened NOW. The Lord began to instruct me on how to play the piano and began teaching me about the connection between praise, worship, and the Glory! It catapulted me into my ministry and launched me into almost forty nations around the world! As you put a demand on eternity, you too will be thrust forward—forward toward what God has for you.

―――――≫≻◦≺≪―――――

When you recognize the realm of eternity is present, press into eternity and suddenly you will unlock the door into the flow of God's blessings.

―――――≫≻◦≺≪―――――

When the disciples did as Jesus instructed, suddenly the water began to turn into supernatural wine! That had never happened before! It was so magnificent that the master of the banquet was baffled that this superior wine had been left until last. Before this time, Jesus had never performed miracles during his earthly ministry. What triggered this sudden miraculous outbreak? You must get this revelation into your spirit: obedience to God's instructions will take you out of time, into the realm of eternal blessing. When the disciples obeyed Jesus' instructions, it created a supernatural portal of blessing and allowed the realities of heaven to become the realities of earth. It was the Glory realm invading the earthly realm. God desires to take you beyond your years—beyond your natural abilities and understanding, beyond your earthly training and experience—but you must be willing to listen to His voice and do whatever He tells you to do. God knows how to get the miracle to you, but you must be willing to receive it!

For we are living a life of faith, and not one of sight. – 2 Corinthians 5:7 (Weymouth)

Prayer For You

Father, in the name of Jesus, I thank You for Your realm of eternity that is filled with revelatory knowledge, unlimited miracles, and endless potential. Right now we ask that you would take us beyond our years of experience, beyond our earthly understanding, and give us a revelation of your Glory. Lord, we desire to see your miracles appear here on the earth even as they already exist in the heavenly realms. We ask for Your divine wisdom, guidance, counsel, and light that would lead us into Your ways and Your truth.

Holy Spirit, we invite You to give unusual instruction that will produce unusual results. We are not satisfied with the status quo, but we want to know You better. We ask that You would take us forward in years, advancing us beyond our natural ability, and that we would be used of You in greater and greater ways. Teach us, train us, speak to us, and instruct us. We want to manifest Your Glory in the earth. In Jesus' name. Amen.

Chapter 5

Restoration
of Years

G od said to His people:
*"I will repay you for the years the
locusts have eaten—the great locust and
the young locust, the other locusts and the locust
swarm." – Joel 2:25*

I just love how God doesn't just restore the years the
locust—or a destroying force—has eaten, but also ensures
us that He'll take care of *every* kind of destroying force that
comes into our lives—the big ones, the little ones, and the
ones that come in swarms!

Praise Your Way to Restoration

Restoration is always connected with praise. Praise will
do things in your life that nothing else can, because instead

of focusing on your problems, you begin to focus on the answer: Jesus Christ!

In Psalm 34:1, David the psalmist is speaking. He says,

I will extol the LORD at all times; his praise will always be on my lips.

That word *praise* is talking about an appraisal. Do you know what an appraisal is? An appraisal is when someone tells you how much something is worth. The appraisal gives worth to something.

When I see that the word *praise* comes from the word for appraisal, then it tells me that God wants to put a praise inside of us, giving value to Him. Our praise should give value to His Glory, should give value to His name.

Let me tell you this about praise. Right now you can give more praise than you could this morning because there is always something new that God has done. The Glory of God is always unfolding.

The Bible talks about the amazing four living creatures in the heavenly dimension. The creatures are covered in eyes and wings, and they have encircled God's throne ever since they were created. Their eyes are open to gaze upon His beauty and majesty, and to gaze upon the revelation of the heavens. Day and night, night and day, they circle the throne. And the only thing that they can say is, "Holy, Holy, Holy!"

All they can see is His beauty, and all they can say is, "Holy, Holy, Holy!" Every time they circle the throne, they see something different about Him that they didn't see the last time they circled. Then they circle again, and there's another part of His character, another piece of His presence, and another element of who He is. And they begin to see and know when the revelation comes.

In the life of every believer, God wants us to increase in our revelation of Him. He desires that we would increase in the revelation of the knowledge of Him. Some of us have known Him as Savior, but now He wants you to know Him as Provider. And some of you have known Him as Provider, and He wants you to know Him as Healer. Some of you have known Him as Healer, but He says, "I am the baptizer in the Holy Spirit." And some of you have known Him as baptizer in the Holy Spirit, but He says, "I want you to know Me as your shelter."

There's always something new to see, and there's always something new to learn. If we get to that place where we think we know it all or we've seen it all, I tell you this, we really haven't seen anything. We really don't know anything at all, because He is so awesome and He is so great!

David the psalmist said, "I will exalt the Lord at all times." This is a praise song. I can't stop praising God today, because there's something new that I'm about to see. I can't just give Him this praise that I'm offering Him right now, because there's another praise that's coming in a few minutes when I see something about Him that I've never seen before. There's something that's bubbling up on the inside because He is so good and He is so awesome. It's a praise that will continually be on my lips.

———◆———

I can't just give Him this praise that I'm offering Him right now, because there's another praise that's coming in a few minutes when I see something about Him that I've never seen before.

———◆———

David went on to say,

> *My soul shall make its boast in the LORD; the humble shall hear of it and be glad. Oh magnify the LORD with me, and let us exalt His name together.* – Psalm 34:2-3 (NKJV)

You know, there's something about your praise. You don't praise because of what you're going through, but you praise because of who He is, what He has done, and what He is about to do. There's something about your praise that becomes like a magnifying glass. David said, *"Oh magnify the Lord with me."*

Praise Magnifies Jesus

When I was in kindergarten, my great-grandfather passed away. He had built a beautiful merry-go-round for my brother and sisters and me, and he put it right in his front yard. It was a large, full-sized merry-go-round. He painted the panels with different nursery rhymes, and he set gospel records to play as it turned. He thought this was the way he could evangelize the whole community. People would want to ride on the merry-go-round and when they got on, they would listen to the gospel records.

He built us this merry-go-round that took up his whole front yard. Every time we went to his house he would seat us in the merry-go-round and give us a big bowl of ice cream. And we would just sit there going around, and around, and being so proud of our great-grandpa.

When he passed away, I was really sad. Some of my relatives told me, "You can go to your great-grandfather's house and pick out whatever you want." I was trying to think of what would remind me of him. I found this tiny little hammer that he had used to build the little delicate pieces of the merry-go-round. So I picked out the hammer and said, "I want this."

Something else I remembered about my grandfather is that he would always read the newspapers. Not only that, but he thought there would be value to a newspaper later on down the road, so he would never get rid of them. After he was done reading the newspaper for the day, he would pack it up until he had newspapers all over his whole house. But in order to read them he always used a magnifying glass.

Now I was in kindergarten and I couldn't read very well. But I tell you, I took that magnifying glass and I found things to do with that magnifying glass that had nothing to do with education or reading. I remember I took it to the schoolyard one day. I snuck it in my backpack. When I had all the kids around me, I pulled it out, and positioned it just right under the sun. We began to burn stuff. Poor little bugs! I noticed that the magnifying glass caused the sunlight to focus like a laser.

David said, *"Oh magnify the Lord with me."* He is telling us that when you praise, you begin to magnify what you praise. When you begin to praise the Lord, you're magnifying the Lord. You're saying that He is bigger than your trouble. You're saying that He is bigger than your circumstances. He's bigger than what you're going through today.

And when you begin to magnify Him, the Bible says that the Son of righteousness is the light. The Son of righteousness shall rise with healing in His wings (Malachi 4:2). When the Son is risen, and you begin to magnify God through praise, His light begins to shine through your praise upon your life, so that your praise will cause things to come into focus. Your praise will cause the light of His Glory to come upon your life and burn out the things that are not of

God, to burn out the things of the enemy, burn out those areas of darkness.

Praise magnifies God, who is the light that shines upon us. His light comes upon the magnifying glass of our praise and brings things into focus. And what is the result? The result is that you might be healed and set free. There's a connection between your praise and the healing that God gives. There's a connection between the praise and the miracles of God. There's a connection between when we praise God and when we receive from God.

Luke 17 tells us the story of the ten lepers. It says that they had been sent away from the village because they had leprosy. But then Jesus came. Luke 17:11-12 says:

> *Now on his way to Jerusalem, Jesus traveled along the border between Samaria and Galilee. As he was going into a village, ten men who had leprosy met him. They stood at a distance and called out in a loud voice, "Jesus, Master, have pity on us!"*

You see, Jesus was their only hope. Medical science had sent them away. The doctors had turned them away. The people—even their families—had turned them away. All they had left was the hope that Jesus would do something.

Some of you reading this are in a situation where everybody has forsaken you. Everybody has turned you away. Doctors and medical science have said there's no cure, there's no help for you, but I tell you this: Jesus Christ, the King of Glory, the King of Righteousness, the King of Kings and the Lord of Lords, is real. He wants to heal you even as you read this book. Don't let Him pass you by. Reach out and touch Him just like the woman with the issue of blood, suffering for all those years in her body. She realized that Jesus was passing by and He was her only hope. She pushed through the crowds; she pushed through the obstacles that were in her way. She touched the hem of His garment and He turned around because He felt healing virtue going out from Him. And He said, "Woman, your faith has made you whole."

Your praise is a sound of faith. Your praise is a sound of victory. When nothing else works, you can always praise Him. When the medicine doesn't work, when the counseling doesn't work, when the accounting just doesn't seem to line up and get straightened out, there's always a praise that that you can release. Hallelujah!

Your praise is a sound of faith. Your praise is a sound of victory. When nothing else works, you can always praise Him.

Praise Releases Healing

Jesus passed by ten lepers one day. The lepers called out, *"Jesus, Master, have pity on us!"* Verse 14 says, *"When he saw them, he said, 'Go, show yourselves to the priests.'"*

Jesus spoke the Word. And I want to tell you this: when God speaks a word, one word from God will change everything. One word from God can entirely change your life. One word from God can bring you from a place of despair to a place of blessing and abundance. One word from God will lift you out of the miry pit, out of that place out of the miry clay, and set your feet on the rock of life. Jesus came to give you life, and to give it more abundantly.

He said, *"Go, show yourselves to the priests."* He spoke the Word. They simply heard the Word, it says, and they obeyed it. They showed themselves to the priests. And as they were obedient to the Word, they were cleansed. And I want you to underline that in your Bible. Get your Bible out right now and underline that phrase. It says that they were cleansed! In some translations it says it says that they were healed. How many were healed? All of them. All ten. What were they healed of? They were healed of the leprosy.

What is leprosy? It is a disease that attacks the extremities and the nervous system of a person. Leprosy numbs all feeling in the body. Someone with leprosy can't feel the touch of another human being. They can't even feel their own fingers and toes. They can't feel their arms or their nose or their hands. There is no feeling in the extremities of the body.

What happens after this is that people with leprosy will injure their fingers or their toes, or ears—you name it. Sometimes they burn themselves. Sometimes they shut doors on their fingers or drop objects on their feet. The damage that comes to these extremities can become so severe that they fall off or begin rotting away; dead pieces of flesh still attached to a living body. It's common for people with leprosy, to be missing fingers or toes. Sometimes they will lose their nose or other parts of their body. Why? The Bible says the enemy comes to steal, to kill, and to destroy (John 10:10). That's the work of the enemy.

We've been India before. We've seen lepers in India and we've seen how leprosy has taken from their body. They're missing all their fingers, their toes, and their nose. Just gone! These people are lying on a cardboard mat in the middle of the road, ready to die. Think about that for a moment!

But Jesus in His power and in the miracle virtue that He was walking in, He spoke the Word, they obeyed the Word. It must have been difficult for them to go. If they were missing toes, they might have walked off balance or had to crawl. We don't know because the Scripture doesn't tell us. But whatever they had to do, they obeyed the Word of God.

The Bible says, *"As they went, they were cleansed."* Cleansed of what? Cleansed of the leprosy. The feeling returned to their bodies. Suddenly, God began to manifest His healing virtue—removing all the leprosy.

The Bible goes on in verse 15, and says, *"One of them* [you can be this one!], *when he saw that he was healed, came back, praising God in a loud voice."*

Now there's the key right there. It doesn't say that he came back with a timid, little thank you. The Bible says that he came back and he was praising God in a loud voice! He recognized who Jesus was. He recognized what Jesus had done in his life.

The Bible says, *"He who began the good work in you is faithful to complete it"* (Philippians 1:6). And *"Every good and perfect gift comes from above"* (James 1:17). God is releasing miracles. God is releasing His healing virtue.

The Voice of Gratitude Restores

I remember several years ago when we were in San Diego, ministering in a church. One of the women in the church was missing all her teeth. She went to a ladies Bible study and prayer meeting on a Thursday morning. Do you know what happened? She got one, pearly white tooth in the middle. It simply grew back: one little white tooth.

Some people would say, "Well that looks foolish," or, "Why would God do that? Why would God just give her one tooth?" I've heard this too, "Well, why would God give gold teeth when people need white teeth? Or why would

God give silver teeth? That's simply a natural fix for the condition." I tell you, I don't care whether God gives gold, silver, blue, purple, or green teeth. The person that had the problem in their mouth does not care either. They are just happy to have their teeth fixed!

Aren't you glad that He's God and we're not? If we were God we might say, "Well, she doesn't deserve that miracle, he doesn't deserve that miracle. I don't think he needs this or that." God is so good. He loves to bless His children. I tell you, He is doing unusual things and He will release signs to make us wonder. He will release signs that catch our attention. Why is he trying to grab our attention? Signs are meant to point us to the very present person of Jesus Christ. When God releases signs people begin thinking about it! They can't stop thinking about what God is doing, what Jesus is saying, and why He's releasing what He's releasing. Signs make us put our focus on Jesus Christ.

You know if He simply gave you a white tooth, you would say, "Well, that's natural. It grew back." I think many times, God does unusual things so we will focus on Him. We will think about Him. His ways are higher than our ways. His thoughts are higher than our thoughts. I tell you, if God is going to give you a whole mouth full of teeth, He's got to start somewhere.

With the woman in that Bible study, He started with one white tooth, right in the front. But He is faithful to finish His work. The Bible says that only one of the lepers came back, praising God in a loud voice. He threw himself at the feet of Jesus and thanked Him, and he wasn't even a Jew; he was a Samaritan.

Jesus asked in verse 17, *"Were not all ten cleansed? Where are the other nine?"* The Bible doesn't tell exactly what happened to other nine. But as I was reading this I realized something. The Bible doesn't say that when Jesus cleansed them of the leprosy that they got all their fingers back. It doesn't say that they got their toes back, their nose back, or their ears back. It just says that they were cleansed.

In other words, the leprosy could not go further. So maybe they were cleansed and they could tell they were cleansed, but they were still missing some fingers. Maybe the one who returned to Jesus had to struggle to get back because he was still missing a few toes. Perhaps he was missing his fingers, or maybe he didn't have his ears or his nose. The Bible doesn't explain it. But he came back to Jesus praising in a loud voice.

Sometimes people think, "Well, I guess this is all that God is going to give me. I guess this is the only miracle He has for me." When God wants to bring forth miracles, signs, and wonders in your life, He has to start somewhere, and He will start with your praise. And as we sow to the heavens, God always sows to the earth. As we lift up a shout of victory there's something that comes from within the cloud of Glory.

One man returned to Jesus, giving praise with a loud voice. God loves your loud praise. The leper threw himself at Jesus' feet. He thanked Him. And Jesus said, *"Were not all ten cleansed? Where are the other nine? Was no one found to return and give praise to God except this foreigner?"*

God is looking for your praise. God is looking for a sound of praise. There's something about your praise that changes the atmosphere. There's something about your praise that causes realms to be moved. There's something about your praise that causes the miracle flow to come. There's something about your praise that causes the signs, wonders, and Glory of God to show up on the scene. Jesus says, "Was no one found to return and give praise except this foreigner?"

Look at what happened next: Jesus said to him, "Rise." Why did he say rise? He said that because the man was on the ground. He said, *"Rise and go; your faith…"*—the sound of praise, the sound of victory—*"has made you whole."* Your faith has made you whole. Whole! Your praise has made you whole. In other words, you are getting your fingers back right now. They are growing in. Right now, your toes are coming back. Look at your nose. Your nose is coming back. You returned with praise and you are being healed.

Praise brings blessings. Where are the other nine? They assumed that was all they were going to receive. Only one person said, "God's not through with me. God's not through blessing me. God's not through doing what only He can do."

He came back praising, and Jesus said, "Rise and go; that sound, that faith, has made you whole."

Your praise does the same thing. It's changing the atmosphere. Your praise is even changing the climate, the temperature, and the health of your body. Your praise is changing things in your family.

Praise God with me. God is working His signs and wonders, and your praise brings back the blessings. Praise brings back what the enemy tried to steal and destroy. Some of you are not missing fingers or toes, but you've been missing family members. For some of you, there are areas of your body where you need healing because the enemy tried to rob you, tried to rip you off. But your praise changes the atmosphere.

Praise God with me. God is working His signs and wonders, and your praise brings back the blessings. Praise brings back what the enemy tried to steal and destroy.

Some of you are looking at your bank account and saying, "This isn't the way it's supposed to be. God, I need a miracle." Lift up that voice of praise. Lift up that voice of faith.

Jesus is saying, "Is there no one to return and give praise? Is there not one to give thanks?"

Testimony of Restoration

As I close this book, I want to share with you an encouraging testimony of God's ability to restore what has been lost—no matter what it is.

During the time we were establishing ministry offices in Palm Springs, California, I couldn't find my wedding band, my pinky ring, or my watch. I looked all over the house. My wife and son looked all over the house. We couldn't find them. I called my secretary and asked her to look in the Canadian office. It was nowhere to be found. I had to leave Canada without these possessions.

We moved into our new location and everything was great—except for the fact that it was our wedding anniversary and I couldn't find my wedding band. Janet Angela and I went out to celebrate and had a fun time, but I didn't have my wedding band. I felt terrible about it.

The next afternoon I was resting in the living room before going out for the evening. Janet Angela was finishing up a few things and our son, Lincoln, was watching some cartoons on the television. I fell asleep and had a dream about being in our offices in Canada. In this dream I received a word of knowledge: the rings and the watch that I had been looking for were in the back of my mailbox in Canada. Still dreaming, I followed this word of knowledge and looked in the mailbox. I saw my wedding band and put it on. I saw my pinky ring and put it on. I saw my watch and put it on my wrist.

All of a sudden the television volume rose dramatically and I was jolted out of my dream. I was irritated, and turned to tell Lincoln to turn down television. Suddenly I caught sight of my hand. I was wearing my wedding band, I was wearing my pinky ring, and I was wearing my watch—in California. In the natural I hadn't gone anywhere. In the natural I was still sitting in my chair in Palm Springs. I had a dream and God began to invade my imagination. I experienced a heavenly download where God began to speak in words of knowledge, and in the Spirit I went out and I got my wedding band, my pinky ring, and my watch. I was so excited! Hallelujah!

A little while later I was ministering in Phoenix and I shared this same testimony. Many people were blessed and encouraged to receive God's unusual miracles. I got home late, unpacked my bags, did my laundry, and then immediately re-packed my suitcases because the next morning I was headed to Iowa City. The next morning when I went to put on my rings, my pinky ring was missing! I realized that I had accidentally left it on the night stand in the hotel in Phoenix. I was so upset. I asked Janet Angela to call the hotel and see if they could find it and send it to us. This was my miracle ring!

I arrived in Iowa and called Janet. She told me that she had spoken with the hotel but that they could not find the ring. I said, "Well, you need to call them back and asked them to have a meeting with all the housekeepers. Not just one of them. Get them all together and confront all of them about this ring because I know exactly where I left this ring—right on the night stand beside the bed." So she called them back and they were gracious enough to gather all the housekeepers together. They talked to them all; each one denied that they had seen the ring. Nobody had the ring. Perhaps one of them didn't clean the room well enough, and the next guest came in and found the ring.

I was upset because this was my miracle ring! I flew home from Iowa, picked up Janet Angela, and we drove to Los Angeles. From there we caught a plane to Fiji before going on to New Zealand to minister. While we were ministering there God spoke to me about sharing the testimony of the rings. I prayed, "God, I can't give that testimony because I don't have the pinky ring. What if the people ask to see the ring?" But God said to do it, so I did it.

Sure enough, after the meeting people said, "Where's the ring? I want to see the pinky ring." I was so embarrassed. I wasn't going to tell them that I was a bad steward of the miracle. I believed for another dream, another word of knowledge, anything in the Spirit so I could go and get it. But the dream didn't come.

Sometimes that happens. You believe for a miracle to come in one form, and it doesn't happen that way. So when the people asked me where the ring was, I said, "Well, I don't have it with me right now." In reality, I didn't have it with me at that moment and I didn't think I would ever have it again. This ring was even more special because it was an inheritance for my son, Lincoln. I was only allowed to wear it until he was old enough that it would fit his finger.

I felt terrible about the loss and began talking to Janet Angela about it. I said, "Where can I go and get another ring that's even half as nice as the ring that I lost?" As I was thinking about this, Janet Angela fell asleep. I was sitting on the bed, trying to think of a place that would give me a good deal—perhaps some discount jewelry store or wholesaler. But I didn't want another ring; I wanted *that* ring. I tossed and turned all night. In the morning I woke up feeling discouraged and disappointed.

Janet Angela was going to minister that morning. I told her, "I'm not going to go. I'm just going to stay here in my pajamas." As I sat in bed thinking about the ring, a picture came to my mind and I began to focus on it. I saw clear image of a house with a front door. I went to the door and walked through it. I turned left inside the house and went through the living room area. Then I turned right and walked through the kitchen and dining room. I turned right again and went down a hallway. On the right I could see the bathroom. On the left there was a bedroom: I looked into that bedroom.

This was all in my mind. I wasn't having a closed vision. I wasn't in a dream or a trance. It was just an idea—a picture in my imagination. I was completely aware that I was still in New Zealand. I could hear the birds outside. I could hear the cars on the street. I knew that I was sitting in the hotel in my pajamas. I was aware of all these things, and at the same time I was focused on the image that the Holy Spirit was putting in my mind.

I looked into that bedroom in my mind and I saw my ring sitting on the dresser. With my physical hand I reached out to grab the ring, and in my mind I saw my hand reaching out to grab the ring as well. As I grabbed a hold of it in my mind, I felt something come into my physical hand. I reached out into my imagination, and experienced God's imagination. God was entertaining my mind. He was entertaining my thoughts. He was downloading pictures from the heavenlies into my mind. I began to see as He was seeing. And I began to do as He was showing me to do. I reached out and grabbed the ring. I felt the ring in my hand. I opened my hand, and my ring was in my hand. While I was sitting in New Zealand, my ring came from North America. My ring had traveled in the Glory realm! There's no distance, no space, no limitation in the Glory of God.

As the ring came into my hand, I quickly shut my eyes again and tried to grab whatever else I could find. But as I shut my eyes, I couldn't see a thing. The "God thoughts" I had been experiencing were gone.

What happens when you begin to get God's thoughts into your thoughts? The Bible is clear that we are to have the mind of Christ (1 Corinthians 2:16; Philippians 2:5). He wants to download His ideas and His creativity. He wants to download the imagination of the heavens into your imagination. He wants to entertain your mind with Glory. He wants you to be transformed by the renewing of your mind (Romans 12:2). He will keep you in perfect peace as your mind is fixed upon Him (Isaiah 26:3). God wants to give you a miracle mindset. I have an entire teaching on this that I would encourage you to get a hold of; it's a wonderful book called *31 Days To A Miracle Mindset*.

A woman in New Zealand heard what God had done with me and got excited because she had lost a beautiful brooch, a family heirloom worth tens of thousands of English pounds. She had lost the brooch ten years prior, while she was still living in the UK. The morning after hearing my testimony, she woke up, and opened the drawer where she sat every morning to do her hair. Sitting right there in that drawer, where she looked every day, was her beautiful brooch. God had returned that family heirloom, that family treasure. The inheritance was recovered and restored!

The God of Time and Eternity

The Bible says that Jesus came to seek and save all that was lost (Luke 19:10). The Father sent His Son from eternity into time to do for us what we could not do for ourselves. He is still doing that today for those who hope in Him. What are you hoping for? God will help you *invest* your time wisely so that you will bear fruit that remains. John 15:16 says:

> *You did not choose me, but I chose you and appointed you so that you might go and bear fruit—fruit that will last—and so that whatever you ask in my name the Father will give you.*

God has chosen you—He has appointed you—to go and bear fruit, eternal fruit. Go forth in Jesus' name and be fruitful with your time for His eternal kingdom.

Remember that there are no limitations in the Spirit. There are no limitations in the Glory realm.

- You can make the most of your time!
- Time can be supernaturally reversed for you!
- You can experience divine favor with time!
- You can move beyond your years into the limitless realm of success!
- God is able to restore everything that the enemy has tried to steal from you!

Dear Friend,

I believe that you are a kingdom connection! God wants to use you to make a difference in the lives of thousands around the world. Do you believe that?

I would like to invite you to become a **Miracle Worker** with me, and help me take this supernatural message of Jesus Christ and His glory to the far corners of the earth.

Partnership is not simply giving of your finances; it is more. When you become a **Miracle Worker** with this ministry, you will become an integral member of the New Wine International outreach ministry team with special opportunities and privileges that will position you to have global impact.

A *"Miracle Worker"* is a person who agrees to:

1. Financially support the ministry of New Wine International (NWI)
2. Pray faithfully for Joshua & Janet Angela Mills and the NWI Ministry Team as they carry the message of Jesus Christ around the world.
3. Pray for those who will receive ministry through NWI ministry events and resources.

Partnership is not only what you can do to help me, but also what I can do to help you. Becoming a **Miracle Worker** with NWI provides a covenant agreement between you and me. By being a **Miracle Worker,** you will connect with the anointing and glory on this ministry as I send you monthly updates and revelatory teachings on the glory realm. You will receive my continued prayer for you and your family and you will be linked with the unique anointing that is on this ministry for unusual signs and wonders.

There are currently several ways to partner with NWI. I want you to decide the partnership level according to what the Lord has placed in your heart to do.

In His Great Love,

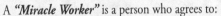

Joshua Mills

P.S. *Call my office today to become a partner or register online so that I can send you a special* **Miracle Worker** *Welcome Package filled with special benefits and information.*

Toll-Free: **1-866-60-NEW-WINE**
Online 24/7:
www.NewWineInternational.org
www.PartnersInPraise.com

Endnotes

1   C. F. Keil, Commentary on the Old Testament, Vol. 1 (Grand Rapids: Wm. B. Eerdmans Publishing Company, 1978), p. 223.

2   Gloria Copeland, *Believers Voice Of Victory* Magazine, June 2010.

3   Gordon Lindsay, The Bible Secret Of Divine Health, Published by Christ For The Nations.

More Resources from Joshua & Janet Angela Mills

For additional copies of this book, more information about live spiritual training seminars, The Intensified Glory Institute®, and other glory resources, please contact the ministry of Joshua & Janet Angela Mills. See page four of this book for our contact information.

Bulk Order Discounts for Ministries, Churches & Christian Retailers

Discounts are available to all churches, ministries and bookstores that desire to place large quantity orders. For more information please email: product@newwineinternational.org

Praise for these Best-selling Books...

"Joshua has identified simple, yet profound keys found in the Word of God that will help the reader receive an impartation to unlock the realms of success and happiness..."

- Drs. Christian & Robin Harfouche (Senior Pastors, Miracle Faith Center, Pensacola, FL)

"...31 Days Of Health, Wealth and Happiness is a helpful resource to assist you in your daily walk of faith... we recommend this book to you!"

- Dr. Stephen & Kellie Swisher (Senior Executives, Kenneth Copeland Ministries)

"...Joshua Mills brings a faith building truth, a scriptural basis for that truth, a great quote for the day and a reminder of Biblical accounts of the miraculous. Each page will move you toward a miracle mindset that will, in turn, catapult you into the glory realm of God...where nothing is impossible. This book is a must read for anyone who wants to live in a greater dimension of the supernatural."

- Dr. Jeff Walker, D. Min., Psy. D., Licensed Clinical Psychologist

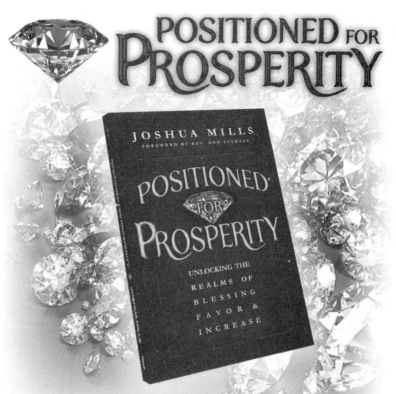

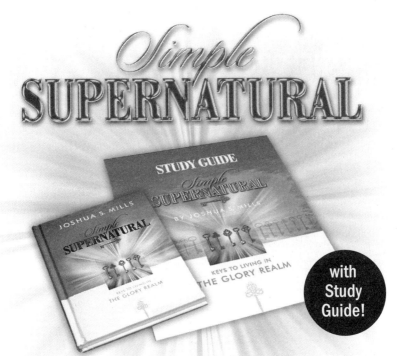